THE REALLY
REALLY
REALLY
EASY STEP-BY-STEP
COMPUTER
BOOK

THE REALLY

REALLY

REALLY

EASY STEP-BY-STEP

COMPUTER

BOOK

**ROBYNN HOFMEYR
AND GAVIN HOOLE**

Recycle Bin

12:00 PM

Reprinted 2006
First published in 2001 by
Struik Publishers
(a division of New Holland Publishing (South Africa) (Pty) Ltd)
Cornelis Struik House
80 McKenzie Street
Cape Town 8001
South Africa

10 9

PUBLISHING MANAGER: Linda de Villiers
EDITOR: Joy Clack
DESIGNER: Beverley Dodd
ILLUSTRATOR: Cheryl Smith

Reproduction by Hirt & Carter Cape (Pty) Ltd
Printed and bound by Times Offset (M) Sdn Bhd

ISBN 1 86872 682 7

Contents and Progress

TICK THINGS OFF AS YOU LEARN THEM ✔

Read this before you start

Welcome to the wonderful and sometimes exasperating world of computers. The purpose of this book is to help you get going with your computer – successfully and fast. There's a minimum of talk and a maximum of getting on with it.

WHAT YOU WILL LEARN FROM THIS BOOK

This book will show you, in clear, easy steps, how to:
- find your way comfortably around your computer;
- create, save and print documents;
- use e-mail to communicate with your family or business colleagues anywhere in the world;
- 'surf the net' to search for information around the world;
- choose a computer if you need to.

There are many books that teach you how to use a particular program in depth. This is not one of them. Within minutes of starting Chapter 1 you'll begin to see that the computer is not a mind-boggling mystery, but a simple yet powerful tool that's as easy to use as a can-opener or spanner.

DON'T SKIP CHAPTERS

It's important for you to know certain things first so that you can successfully learn others that follow. Start at the beginning and don't skip any chapters along the way, because each chapter builds on the knowledge gained in earlier chapters.

So, let's go!

1 Getting started

SWITCHING ON YOUR COMPUTER

Right. First of all you need to switch the thing on.

1. Look on the big box (sometimes called the **tower**) for something that looks like a power-on switch. Usually it's the type of switch you push in.
2. Switch on. When you hear a sound like an aeroplane taking off, that's it, you're on your way.

3. Wait while it gets its act together (called **booting up**), and when it settles down your screen should look similar to one of those pictured below. (Don't worry if it's not exactly the same as this, as every computer is a bit different.)

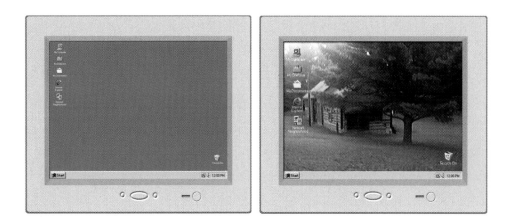

USING THE MOUSE

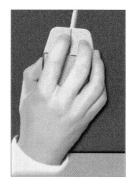

Now is a good time to tell you how to use your **mouse**. The cord comes out of the top, away from you (unless you have one of the modern cordless models).

1. With the cord pointing away from you (unless you have one of the cordless models), rest your index finger and your middle finger on the left and right buttons respectively, with your wrist resting comfortably on the table, as depicted in the illustration above.
2. Relax your hand completely.
3. Move the mouse gently and slowly in a little circle on the special mat (called a **mouse pad**). You'll see that the arrow on the screen (called the **cursor**) also moves around.
4. Spend a few minutes practising this – slowly and carefully – until you get the hang of it.

THE 'DESKTOP'

The screen you're looking at (like those illustrated at the top of this page) is known as the **desktop**. Just as your real desktop has your equipment on it, so this computer desktop shows you all sorts of things you can use. Many are tidied away behind the **Start** button in the bottom left-hand corner. Let's investigate.

OPENING (LOADING) A PROGRAM

We're going to open (load) the program we use to write a document. It's called **Microsoft Word** (or **MS Word**, or **Word**).

---

1. Moving your mouse slowly and carefully, move the arrow onto the **Start** button in the bottom left-hand corner of the screen.
2. Gently press and release the left-hand button on your mouse (this is called **left clicking**).

Your screen should now look like this:

---

3. Move the arrow onto **Programs** in the list and click the left mouse button again.

Your screen should show this menu:

---

4. Choose (point and click on) **Microsoft Word**.
5. Wait a few seconds while **Word** opens up on your screen.

Fantastic! You've just loaded your first computer program. Well done. Your screen should now look like this:

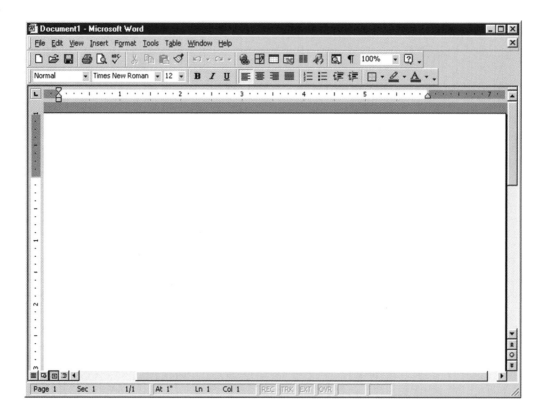

CLOSING (SHUTTING DOWN) A PROGRAM

Let's see how to close a program. Do you see that little box with a **X** in it in the top right-hand corner? The very top one? That's your way to close the program.

1. Click on the **X** and you're back to your desktop. Well done.

Let's just practise that once more. We'll open and close **Word** again, as follows:

1. Click on **Start** (bottom left-hand corner).
2. Choose **Programs**, then **Microsoft Word**.
3. Wait while it opens ... you're in.
4. Click on the little **X** (top right-hand corner). You're out. Done.

FILLING THE WHOLE SCREEN

Sometimes you may find that when you open a program it seems about half the normal size and doesn't fill your screen.

Don't panic, you can fix that easily like this:

1. Look at the top right-hand corner of the program. Do you see the three little buttons there?
2. To **maximize** to full-screen view, click on the button with the line at the top of the little square ▣ . **Word** will now fill the screen.

MINIMIZING A PROGRAM

If you want to leave a program temporarily to do something else, but know that you'll return to it later, you can **minimize** it. This means that the program is actually still open, but is not visible on the screen. Do it like this:

1. Look again at the three buttons in the top right-hand corner of the program.
2. Click on the button with the little line at the bottom ▬ .

3. It should now look as if your program has closed down. Actually, it hasn't.
4. Look at the bottom of your screen. Do you see a button labelled **Document1 - Microsoft Word**?
5. Click on it and **Word** will reappear on your screen.

WHAT IS 'WINDOWS'?

The system you have been using to open and close programs, and so on, is called Microsoft Windows. Soon you'll see that it's possible to work in one program and be able to look into another program at the same time, hence the name Windows – the ability to see into several programs simultaneously.

WHEN TO SHUT DOWN YOUR PC (PERSONAL COMPUTER)

If you're going to be using your PC intermittently during the day, it's best to leave it switched on, as more wear and tear is likely to take place if you switch it on and off every time you use it. You can just switch it off at night.

! **Never switch off the computer without going through the proper 'Shut down' procedure described on the following page, or you could mess up some settings and data.**

SHUTTING DOWN YOUR COMPUTER

1. Click on **Start** (bottom left-hand corner).
2. Click on **Shut down**.

The following menu will appear:

3. Click on **Shut down**.
4. Click on **OK**.

Your computer will now reorganize itself before shutting down. This is very valuable for you, as if you have done anything odd to upset it, it will now fix things up for you so that you can start with a clean slate when you next switch on.

5. As soon as it has finished this task, the following message will appear on your screen:

6. Switch off (main button on tower). (Some of the newer models even do this for you.)

Now that you know how to open and close programs, you are ready to move on to Chapter 2, where you will learn how to use one of these programs to do some work.

2 Writing a document

The computer's version of good old pen and paper is a word processing program such as **Microsoft Word** (or **Word** for short). So before you begin, you must first open **Word**.

OPENING MICROSOFT WORD

1. Click on **Start** (bottom left-hand corner).
2. Choose (click on) **Programs**, then **Microsoft Word**.

That's it, you're in. Your screen should look something like this:

TYPING

If you're new to typing, try the following exercises to familiarize yourself with the keyboard and some of its functions.

1. Type your first name (don't bother about capitals yet).
2. To make a space, press the long **spacebar** that runs along the bottom of the keyboard.
3. Type your surname.
4. Press the Backspace key several times to delete your name letter by letter.

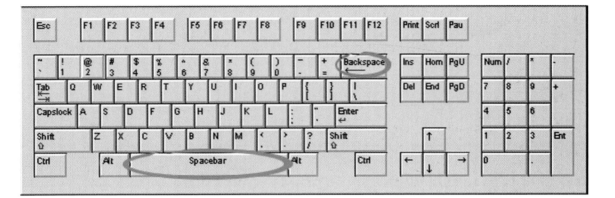

5. Type and erase your name several times until you feel comfortable with the keys.
6. Now CAPITALS: to make a capital letter, hold down one of the Shift keys, and lightly tap the letter you want to type.

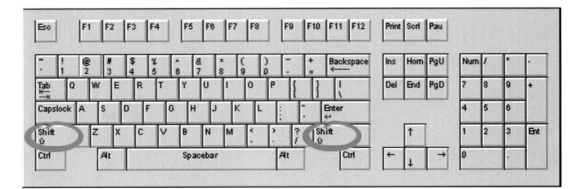

Note: Some keyboards have the word **Shift**; others just have an arrow ⇧.

Now type as follows:

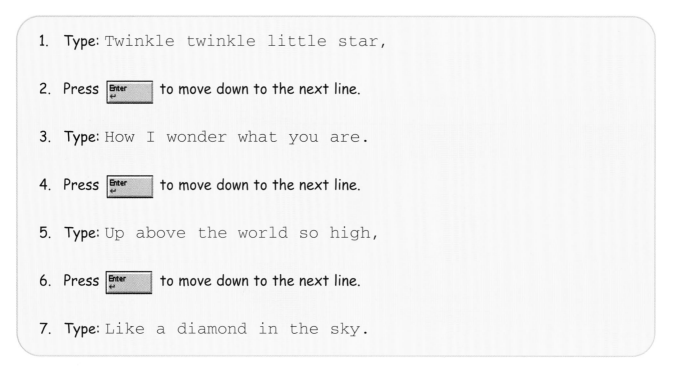

1. Type: Twinkle twinkle little star,

2. Press [Enter] to move down to the next line.

3. Type: How I wonder what you are.

4. Press [Enter] to move down to the next line.

5. Type: Up above the world so high,

6. Press [Enter] to move down to the next line.

7. Type: Like a diamond in the sky.

TYPING A PARAGRAPH

Before you start

Notice that when you reach the end of a line, the computer automatically 'wraps' around to the beginning of the next line for you. You mustn't tell the computer when to do this; it will happen automatically.

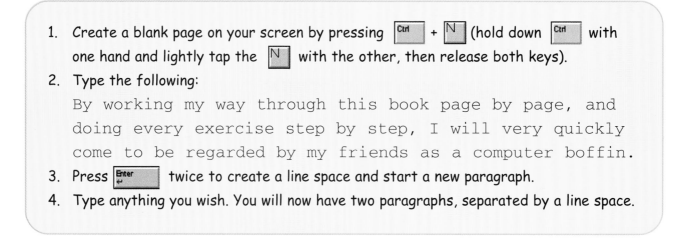

1. Create a blank page on your screen by pressing [Ctrl] + [N] (hold down [Ctrl] with one hand and lightly tap the [N] with the other, then release both keys).
2. Type the following:
   By working my way through this book page by page, and doing every exercise step by step, I will very quickly come to be regarded by my friends as a computer boffin.
3. Press [Enter] twice to create a line space and start a new paragraph.
4. Type anything you wish. You will now have two paragraphs, separated by a line space.

SAVING A FILE (DOCUMENT)

To practise, let's pretend you need to store this document safely for future use.

1. Press `Ctrl` + `S` .

Your screen should look like this:

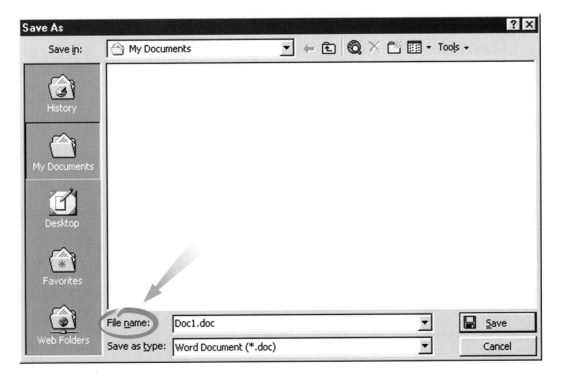

See the words **File name:** followed by a white box? This is called a window.

2. Type in a name for this file – let's call it **retire** – and the computer will automatically position it for you in the window.

It's important to keep your file names short and to the point so that you'll be able to easily recognize them in future.

3. Click on **Save** (on the right of the window).

That's it. You've just saved your first computer file.

Look at the top left-hand corner of your screen – see **retire** up there? This is useful for knowing which file you're working in if you become distracted.

> **SAVE FREQUENTLY!**
>
> It's *very* important to get into the habit of saving your file regularly as you go along, so that if there is a power failure or something goes wrong you won't lose your work. Saving after every few paragraphs is a good habit to cultivate. Once a file has a name, the **Save As** window won't appear when you press `Ctrl` + `S` , but the computer will nevertheless update your file in the background as you go on with your work.

CLOSING A FILE

When you're finished with your document, you can close it like this:

1. Look at the list of words near the top of the screen starting with <u>F</u>ile, <u>E</u>dit, <u>V</u>iew, etc. This is called the **Menu bar**.
2. Click on **<u>F</u>ile** and watch a menu appear.
3. Click on **<u>C</u>lose**.

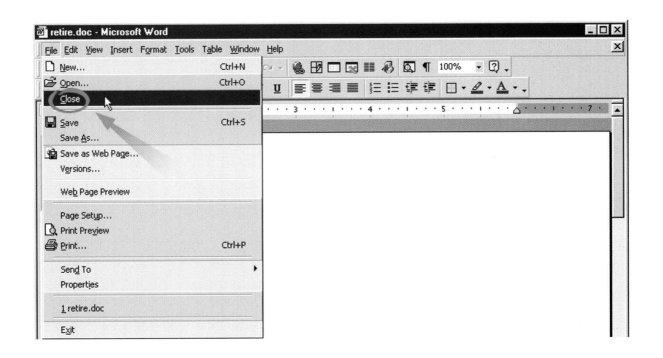

It's as easy as that.

OPENING AN EXISTING FILE

1. Click on **File**.
2. Click on **Open**.

Your computer will bring up your list of files, and your screen will look something like this (take note that the file name now has **.doc** behind it to indicate that it is a **Word** document):

3. Click on the file you wish to open.
4. Click on **Open** (on the right of the window).

PRINTING A FILE

Make sure that the printer is plugged in and switched on and that there is paper in the tray.

1. Press `Ctrl` + `P` (hold down `Ctrl` with one hand and then lightly tap `P` with the other. Release both keys). The following window will open.
2. Press `Enter`.

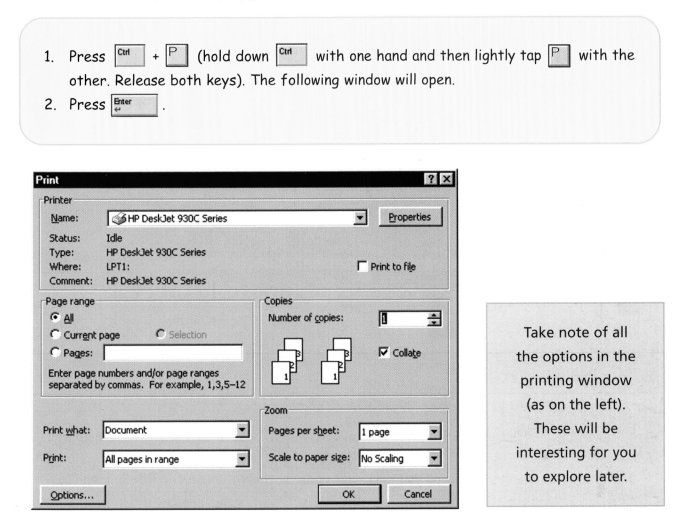

Take note of all the options in the printing window (as on the left). These will be interesting for you to explore later.

Congratulations – you've just printed your first computer document. Well done!

A note about choices

With computers there are often several different ways to do the same thing. For example, to print a document, you could:

- Press `Ctrl` + `P` ; or
- In the **Menu bar** click on **File**, then **Print**; or
- Click on the **Print icon** in the **Toolbar**.

As you become more experienced, you will learn how to use the various options, but in this book we decided to keep things simple in order to avoid confusion. We have generally used the options that most beginners find the easiest to understand.

Highlighting a line

1. Move your cursor to the left-hand margin alongside the line you wish to highlight. The cursor will change shape and direction like this:

 Mary had a little lamb

2. Click once and the whole line will be highlighted.

Highlighting a paragraph

1. Move your cursor to the left-hand margin alongside the paragraph you wish to highlight. The cursor will change shape and direction like this:

   Mary had a little lamb. Its fleece was white as snow. Everywhere that Mary went, her little lamb was sure to go. What a silly lamb.

2. Double-click and the whole paragraph will be highlighted like this.

Highlighting a whole document
This is the easiest of all.

1. Press `Ctrl` + `A` . (A for All.)

COPYING AND MOVING TEXT

This is a very useful feature that helps you to copy or move text from one place to another – even between different programs.

Here's how it works.

---

1. Type the following text:

Did you know that, out of 100 people born in the same year as you, and looking forward to retirement at the age of 65, 49 will be dependent on family, friends or charity, 29 will be dead, 12 will be dead broke, 5 will be forced to continue working, 4 will be financially independent and 1 will be rich. This is something to think about.

2. Press `Enter` several times at the end of the paragraph.

Making a copy of this paragraph

1. Move your cursor to the left-hand margin alongside the paragraph and double-click to highlight it.
2. To copy the paragraph temporarily into the computer's memory, press `Ctrl` + `C`.
3. To insert the copied paragraph elsewhere, click the cursor where you want the copy to appear.
4. Press `Ctrl` + `V`. (Think of **V** as an arrow pointing to where you want the paragraph to appear.) The copy will now be 'pasted' where you wanted it.

Changing the font

1. Click on **Format** in the menu bar.
2. Select **Font**.

This **Font** selection box should appear on your screen:

3. Scroll through the various options in the **Font** window (using your up [↑] and down [↓] arrows) until a font you like is highlighted.
4. Click in the **Font style** box on one of the options offered, and again scroll up and down until a style you like is highlighted.
5. Repeat this for the font **Size** options too, and select any other options you may want to use.

Now, you have a choice to make. Do you want to choose this font for only this document, or would you like the computer to use this font automatically for all your future documents (until you decide to change it again)?

6. If you want to use the font for only this document, click on **OK**.

7. If you want to use the font for all future documents, click on **<u>D</u>efault** (left corner), then **Yes**.

TYPING IN COLOUR

Starting the colour

1. Click on the little down arrow on the right of the $\mathbf{A}$ in the formatting toolbar, as shown below.

2. Click on a colour from the chart that pops up. Whatever you type will now be in this colour.

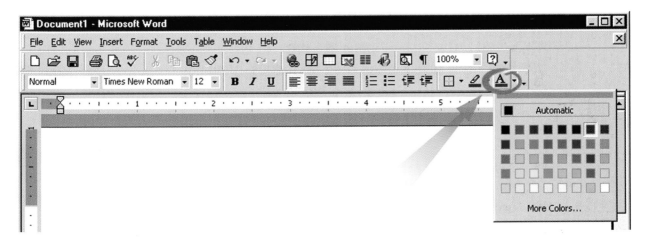

Returning to black

1. Click again on the little down arrow on the right of the $\mathbf{A}$ in the formatting toolbar.

2. Click on the **Automatic** square.

INSERTING PAGE NUMBERS

Word does a great job of doing this for you automatically, once you have told it how you like things to be done.

1. Click on **Insert**, then **Page Numbers**. The following should appear on your screen:

2. Click on the little drop down arrow in the **Position** window, and choose whether you want the page numbers to be at the top or the bottom of the pages.
3. Click on the little drop down arrow in the **Alignment** window, and select one. If you're not sure what you're being offered, then watch the diagram on the right of that window and see what happens to the little black page numbers.
4. Take note of the little white box in the bottom left-hand corner. If it has a tick in it, then there will be a number on the front page, which you may or may not want. Therefore, a tick = number on page one, no tick = no page number on page one. Adjust accordingly by clicking the little window, if necessary.
5. Click on **OK**.

CHECKING YOUR SPELLING

Yes, it's true. **Word** actually checks your spelling for you (and in some versions even your grammar). If you have been wondering why some of your words are underlined with wavy lines, this is the reason.

Checking individual words

1. Type exactly as follows (mistakes and all): `The rane in spain falls manely on the weekends.`
2. Right click (that means click the right-hand button on your mouse) on the word `rane`. (If your spellcheck is set to 'automatic' then this word will have a wavy line underneath it.)
3. Your screen should look like this:

4. Click on **rain** in the list.
5. **Word** will now replace the old, incorrect spelling with the new, correct spelling.
6. Fix the other mistakes in the same way.

Your screen should look something like the example below. If it's very different, now is the time to set up your e-mail properly by following the instructions on page 56 as mentioned above.

2. Click on **New Mail** (or **Compose Mail** in some versions).

Your screen should look something like this:

3. Notice that your cursor is flashing in the **To** window, so type in the e-mail address of the person you wish to write to. Be careful here. E-mail addresses have to be perfectly accurate, so type it in exactly, with no extra capitals or spaces or dots. If you don't have an address handy you can send mail to **robynn@iafrica.com** (be sure to notice the double n in robynn and the i before africa).

4. Now, press [Tab] (or click) to move your cursor to the **Subject** window.

5. Type a couple of words to indicate what your letter is about.

6. Press [Tab] (or click) to move the cursor to the big window.

7. Type your actual letter. Here you can type freely.

8. When your letter is complete, click on **Send** in the toolbar at the top. (This places your letter into the **Outbox** where it will wait until you are ready to actually send the letter - you may have other letters to type.)

9. If your spelling checker comes up at this point, follow the prompts until it disappears.

10. When you're ready to send the letter, click on **Send/Recv** in the top toolbar.

11. If a box comes up asking you to type in your password, do so and then click on **Connect**.

12. You may now hear strange noises, which indicate that your computer is connecting to your service provider.

13. Watch the information box that shows you what is happening – it is sometimes too quick to see.

14. When the information box disappears, this means that your **Send and Receive** is complete. Check that you have disconnected automatically, as outlined below. If you haven't disconnected, then adjust your settings as explained on page 59.

That's it. Well done – you've just sent your first e-mail successfully.

NOTE:
Clicking on **Send/Recv** sends any letters that have been waiting in the **Outbox** and simultaneously brings in any letters that may have been waiting to come in (from other people to you). This new mail will now appear in your **Inbox**.
The letters that have been sent, move from your **Outbox** into **Sent Items**. If you click on **Sent Items**, you will see them listed there, on the right.

HOW TO TELL WHETHER YOU'RE CONNECTED OR NOT

While you are connected, your phone line is in use. To check whether you are connected, do the following:

1. Look in the bottom right-hand corner of your screen. If you are connected you will see two little green screens as illustrated below.

2. To disconnect, right click on the green screens.
3. Click on **Disconnect**.
4. Check that the screens disappear.

READING YOUR MAIL

All mail that is sent to you goes into your **Inbox**. To read your mail, do the following:

1. Click on **Inbox** on the left.

Your screen should look something like this:

2. Click on any of the letters in the list on the right.
3. Press ⌷Enter⌷ to open the letter.
4. Use the up and down arrows on your keyboard to read the letter, if necessary.
5. Press ⌷Esc⌷ to return to the list.

MANAGING YOUR MAIL

Now that you know how to read and write mail, let's get a bit more sophisticated. You may enjoy some of these features.

ORGANIZING YOUR MAIL

Just as you have a system for dealing with your paper mail, you can do the same with your e-mail. Basically, when a letter arrives for you, you probably want to do one of the following with it:
- throw it away;
- reply to it;
- forward it to other people;
- keep it handy for later; or
- file it for future reference.

THROWING MAIL AWAY

This is really easy. Simply:

1. Highlight the letter in the list (click on it once).
2. Press `Del` on your keyboard.

REPLYING TO A LETTER

1. Either have the appropriate letter on the screen or highlight it in the list.
2. Click on **Reply** in the top toolbar. (**Reply** sends mail only to the person who actually sent you the letter. **Reply All** sends copies of your reply to everyone who received the letter along with you. Be sure that you want this to happen before selecting this option.)
3. Notice that the original sender's details are automatically filled in for you, along with the subject.
4. Type your reply.
5. Click on **Send**, then **Send/Recv**.

FORWARDING MAIL TO OTHERS

1. Either have the appropriate letter on the screen or highlight it in the list.
2. Click on **Forward** in the top toolbar.
3. Fill in the e-mail address/es in the **To** window – remember to be accurate.
4. Make any changes to the letter, if necessary.
5. Click on **Send**, then **Send/Recv**.

SENDING MAIL TO MORE THAN ONE PERSON

1. In the **To** window, type the address of the first person, then type a comma, then the address of the next person, then a comma, etc. You may have up to 50 addresses per letter.
2. An alternative is to have only one address in the **To** window and list all the others in the **Cc** window.

3. Use your ⌨[Tab] key (or click) to move from one window to the next, and fill in the person's details. All you really need is their name and e-mail address.

4. Click on **Add**, then **OK**.

ATTACHING DOCUMENTS

This part is more advanced, but is really quite simple to do. Clearly, if you're just chatting to someone or communicating informally you will use the mail as above. But the time will come when you will want to send a more formal document, or perhaps one which you have already created in **Word**.

1. Start as usual, as if you were going to send the person an ordinary e-mail: click on **New Mail**, then fill in the **To** and **Subject** windows.

2. Click on **Attach** in the top toolbar.

3. Click on **My Documents**, then **Attach**.

4. Click on the file you wish to attach, then click on **Attach**.

5. Notice that the file name has been inserted into a new window called **Attach**.

6. Click on **Send**, then **Send/Recv**.

It's as easy as that.

READING AN ATTACHED FILE

This is the same as the above, but in reverse. You will know that an e-mail has an attached file either because the person will tell you in their letter, or because the letter has a little paperclip next to it in the list.

1. Highlight the letter in the list (click on it once).
2. Press ⌷Enter to open the letter.
3. Right click on the name of the attached file in the window labelled **Attach**.
4. Click on **Open**.
5. If a box comes up asking whether you would like to open the file or save it to disk, click on **Open it** and then on **OK**.
6. To close the file when you are done, click on the [X] in the top right-hand corner of the open window.

FREQUENTLY ASKED QUESTIONS ABOUT E-MAIL

1. **How do I know that a letter has actually been sent?**
    Click on **Sent Items** (on the left). The letter should appear in the list on the right.

2. **How do I know what my e-mail address and password are?**
    Ask your service provider and then write them down on page 77.

3. **Who is my service provider?**
    The company you pay monthly to access the Internet. Write down their details on the inside front cover of this book.

4. **How can I check my spelling before I send mail?**
    Press **F7** before sending, or follow the instructions on page 58 to have this happen automatically.

5. **How do I find my way around the keyboard?**
    Do Chapters 1 and 2 of this book.

6. **Why haven't I received mail for ages?**
    When last did you do a **Send and Receive**?

7. **How do I find out someone's e-mail address?**
    Phone and ask them, then add it into your e-mail address book for future use and/or write it down on page 77.

SETTING UP YOUR E-MAIL

For your own maximum efficiency in e-mail usage and to be able to follow the e-mail chapter easily, your e-mail needs to be set up in a particular way.

Actually this is pretty simple stuff, so you have two options, either:

• call the person who usually helps you with your computer and ask them to set you up according to the following pages, or
• be brave and do it yourself. You should be fine if you follow slowly, step by step.

Set up your e-mail as follows:

1. Click on **Start** then **Programs**, then **Outlook Express** to open the e-mail program.
2. Click on **Tools** (in the top menu bar) and then on **Options**.

Your screen should look something like this:

3. Look at the tabs available and click on **General**.
4. If you click on the little windows, ticks will appear or disappear. Adjust them so that the only two windows ticked are:

   ☑ **When starting, go directly to my 'Inbox' folder**, and

   ☑ **Play sound when new messages arrive**

   The others must be unticked, just like the screen shown below.

Options

Tabs: Security | Connection | Maintenance
General | Read | Send | Compose | Signatures | Spelling

General
- ☑ When starting, go directly to my 'Inbox' folder
- ☐ Notify me if there are any new newsgroups
- ☐ Automatically display folders with unread messages
- ☐ Automatically log on to MSN Messenger Service

Send / Receive Messages
- ☑ Play sound when new messages arrive
- ☐ Send and receive messages at startup
- ☐ Check for new messages every [30] minute(s)

   If my computer is not connected at this time:

   [Do not connect]

Default Messaging Programs

This application is NOT the default Mail handler   [Make Default]

This application is NOT the default News handler   [Make Default]

[OK] [Cancel] [Apply]

5. Now click on the **Read** tab.
6. Click on the windows until all of them are unticked, as in the screen on the right.

Options

Tabs: Security | Connection | Maintenance
General | Read | Send | Compose | Signatures | Spelling

Reading Messages
- ☐ Mark message read after displaying for [5] second(s)
- ☐ Automatically expand grouped messages
- ☐ Automatically download message when viewing in the Preview Pane
- ☐ Show ToolTips in the message list for clipped items

   Highlight watched messages with the color [Default ▼]

News
- ☐ Get [300] headers at a time
- ☐ Mark all messages as read when exiting a newsgroup

Fonts

Click here to change the fonts and default encoding used when reading messages

[Fonts...]   [International Settings...]

[OK] [Cancel] [Apply]

7. Click on the **Send** tab.

8. By clicking on the windows, select the options so that it looks like the screen below.

```
Options                                                   ? X
  Security          Connection              Maintenance
General    Read    Send    Compose   Signatures   Spelling

Sending
   [✓] Save copy of sent messages in the 'Sent Items' folder
   [ ] Send messages immediately
   [✓] Automatically put people I reply to in my Address Book
   [✓] Automatically complete e-mail addresses when composing
   [ ] Include message in reply
   [ ] Reply to messages using the format in which they were sent
                                        [ International Settings... ]

Mail Sending Format
   (•) HTML          [ HTML Settings... ]  [ Plain Text Settings... ]
   ( ) Plain Text

News Sending Format
   ( ) HTML          [ HTML Settings... ]  [ Plain Text Settings... ]
   (•) Plain Text

                    [   OK   ]  [ Cancel ]  [ Apply ]
```

9. Leave the **Compose**, **Signatures** and **Security** sections alone. (Trust us, you don't want to mess with this.)

10. Click on the **Spelling** tab.

11. Choose the options as shown on the screen below.

```
Options                                                   ? X
  Security          Connection              Maintenance
General    Read    Send    Compose   Signatures   Spelling

Settings
   [✓] Always check spelling before sending
   [✓] Suggest replacements for misspelled words

When checking spelling, always ignore
   [ ] Words in UPPERCASE
   [✓] Words with numbers
   [ ] The original text in a reply or forward
   [✓] Internet Addresses

Language
   [ English (United Kingdom)          ▼ ]  [ Edit custom dictionary ]

                    [   OK   ]  [ Cancel ]  [ Apply ]
```

12. Click on the **Connection** tab.

13. Make sure there is a tick in both windows as shown below.

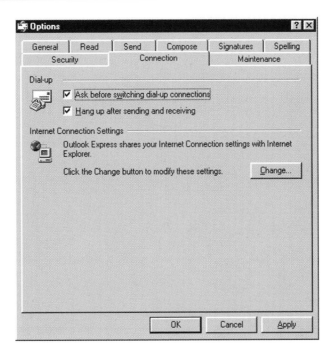

14. Click on the **Maintenance** tab.

15. Select the options so that your screen matches the screen below.

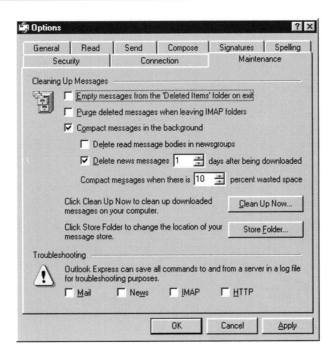

16. To make your changes take effect, click on the **Apply** button and then on the **OK** button.

Well done – you now have a highly efficient, streamlined e-mail system that will also save you money by automatically ensuring that you read and write letters without being connected to the phone line and that, if you forget to disconnect, this will automatically be taken care of.

Now, there's one last thing to do if you want to have the most useful, efficient layout on your screen, so:

17. Click on **View** and then on **Layout**.
18. Select the options to match the screen below.

A FINAL WORD OF ADVICE

You may find friends saying that they have a feature which allows them to see a little window into each e-mail letter without actually loading it onto the screen. This is the **Preview Pane** referred to in the screen picture above. The reason we have set you up so that you **do not** have this feature is because this is a prime way for viruses to load themselves onto your system without your being able to control them. Without the preview pane enabled, you are in full control of which mail you choose to open and which you choose to delete without opening.

Our advice is to open only mail that comes from senders you recognize and to delete all unrecognized mail without opening it.

4 The Internet

WHAT IS THE INTERNET?

In a nutshell, you could think of the Internet as thousands of computers around the world, linked to one another via phone lines. Anyone can connect to this world wide web of computers.

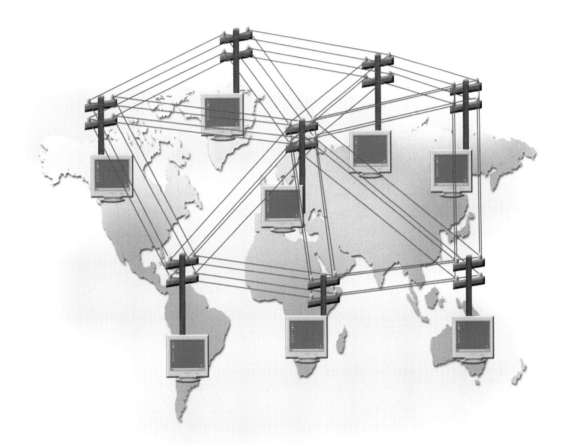

Instead of becoming embroiled in technical details, let's get practical straight away so that you can see for yourself how it works.

There are basically two things Internet beginners want to do:

1. go to a specific website; or
2. search for information about a particular topic.

GOING TO A SPECIFIC WEBSITE

1. Find out the web address of a site you wish to visit. This usually begins with **www**. If necessary, phone the organization or company and ask them for their website address. Write down the address in the space on page 77.
2. Click on **Start**, then **Programs**, then **Internet Explorer**.
3. If you are asked to enter your password, type it in and then click on **Connect**. (Your computer may do this step for you automatically, depending on how it has been set up.)
4. Wait while your computer connects you to the Internet.

The top part of your screen will look something like the illustration below, although the rest could have anything on it, depending on how your computer has been set up.

5. Now, tell your computer which site you wish to visit. For this exercise we'll visit CNN's website.

6. Click anywhere in the **Address** window (see page 62).

7. Press your End key (to get to the end of the line).

8. Press Backspace slowly and carefully to erase whatever address is in the window. Only erase what appears after the **www.**

9. Type in **cnn.com** (the whole address should read **http://www.cnn.com**). Website addresses must be accurate, so be careful to use the correct case of letters (either capitals or lower case) and put in all full stops, including the one after the **www.**

10. Press Enter .

11. Wait while **Internet Explorer** opens this site for you – be patient, this could take a while.

Your screen should now show the CNN site or home page, which changes from day to day, but will look something like this:

MOVING AROUND AN INTERNET SITE

1. Once the site is open, browse around the page using one of several methods:
   - use the scroll bar on the right (click on the little button and drag it up and down with your mouse); or
   - click on the scroll bar arrows; or
   - click in an empty space on the page with your mouse and then simply use your arrows on your keyboard to get around.
2. Take note that some text is blue and/or underlined and that your cursor turns into a hand when it hovers over the text.
3. Click on this type of text and watch as you are taken to another 'page' for more detail on that particular issue.
4. If you wish you hadn't gone there, click on the **Back** icon in the top toolbar to get back to where you were last.

And so on and so forth. Can you see why people get so absorbed in the Internet that they lose all track of time?

While you're 'on-line', you're connected by phone line to the Internet. Some countries charge for these calls, so you may prefer to 'surf the net' during off-peak hours.

DISCONNECTING FROM THE INTERNET

1. Look at the bottom right-hand corner of your screen. If you are connected you will see two small green screens as illustrated below left.
2. To disconnect, right click (click the right button on your mouse) on the green screens.

3. Click on **Disconnect**.
4. Check that the computer screens disappear.

SEARCHING FOR INFORMATION ON THE WEB

This can be done in so many different ways, but let us show you a relatively easy method.

The good news is that there are special Internet sites (called **search engines**) that exist specifically to help you do searches. One of the most popular of these is called **Yahoo!**.

Now, let's assume that you want to find information about where you can swim with dolphins and you have no idea where such information is to be found. You can use the **Yahoo!** search engine to help you find this information.

1. If you're not already connected to the Internet, click on **Start**, **Programs** then **Internet Explorer** to open the program.
2. If you are asked for a password, type it in and press ⌨ Enter . (This step may be done automatically for you.)
3. When the **Address** window appears, type in **Yahoo!'s** address, which is **http://www.yahoo.com** (remember to be accurate about no capitals and exact spelling).

The top of your screen should look something like this:

4. Press ⌨ Enter and wait while the **Yahoo!** site opens up.
5. When it is open, click in the white **Search** window and type "swim with dolphins" (the double quotes must be typed in to narrow down the search).
6. Click on **Search** next to the window (see page 66).
7. Wait while the Internet searches for sites that contain the words you have typed.

Yahoo! - Microsoft Internet Explorer

File   Edit   View   Favorites   Tools   Help

Back   Forward   Stop   Refresh   Home   Search   Favorites   History   Mail

Address   http://www.yahoo.com

HELPFUL TIP FOR SEARCHING:

It's important to type in enough key words so that you narrow down the search to give you relevant results without narrowing it down so much that you get no information at all. You'll soon get the feel of it.

8.   When the search is over, explore the various options you have been offered.

9.   When you find one that looks like it might be what you're looking for, click on the blue underlined text and you'll be taken further along that route.

10. Remember to click on **Back** (top toolbar) when you want to return to the previous page.

REMEMBERING A SPECIFIC SITE

Sometimes you'll find a site so interesting or useful that you'll want to return there time and again. Is there a way to mark that site so that your computer can take you straight there? The answer is Yes! It's called **Favorites**

As the **Yahoo!** search engine is so useful, you'll probably want to use it often, so let's put it into your **Favorites** list as follows:

1. Go to the **Yahoo!** site again (you may still have it loaded, otherwise load it again, as you did before).
2. In the top menu bar, click on **Favorites**.

The following screen should appear:

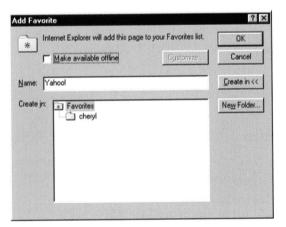

3. Click on **Add to Favorites**, and another menu will pop up:

4. Click on **OK**.
5. Take note that the **Yahoo!** site has now been added to your **Favorites** list.

GETTING TO ONE OF YOUR FAVOURITE SITES

1. Click on **F<u>a</u>vorites** in the top menu bar. Your list should appear.
2. Click on the site you wish to go to.

SOME USEFUL SITES TO EXPLORE

More search engines

www.google.com (an excellent one)

www.altavista.com

www.go.com

www.looksmart.com

www.aardvark.co.za

This book's website

www.avp.co.za/book.html

Buy books and stuff on-line

www.amazon.com

A useful, fast communication service

www.icq.com

Database of newspapers worldwide

www.newsrack.com

Help with computer viruses

www.getvirushelp.com

Useful motoring information and websites

www.passyourlearnerseasily.com

Live African wildlife video-cams

www.africam.co.za

Social site for seniors

www.50plusfriends.com

GOODBYE FROM US

Well, that's the end of the actual teaching in this book. The next chapter is only for those of you who still need to buy a computer.

We've really enjoyed writing the book, and hope you've enjoyed using it. If you'd like to write to us with your comments, you can do this using your newly acquired e-mail skills. Send an e-mail to **robynn@iafrica.com** or **gavin104471@icqmail.com** (we'd love to hear from you).

You can also visit our website at **www.avp.co.za/book.html** for updates and additional useful information.

Have fun!

5 Choosing a computer

> **NB: This chapter is not necessarily for you.**
>
> You have the option of simply walking into a computer shop and asking them to help you to choose a computer that will enable you to:
> - create documents; and
> - use e-mail and the Internet.
>
> If this the best option for you, then you don't need to read this chapter. However, if you are interested in the technicalities and want more details, here they are.

MAKING SOME BASIC DECISIONS

Buying a computer is something like buying a car. There are some basic decisions to consider before you start to shop around, for instance:

- How much can I afford?
- Do I want a new one or a second-hand one?
- Should I buy from a chain store or a computer shop?
- What do I want to do on the computer?
- How powerful should it be?

New or second-hand?

Companies often upgrade their computers, so the old ones become available at good prices. But make sure you're buying from a reputable supplier and try to get some assurance of after-sales service, and perhaps even a guarantee. The danger of buying a second-hand computer is that there is no one to help you when things go wrong – and, with computers, things DO go wrong.

Buying a new computer means you have the latest equipment and program versions (an important consideration with computers) and that when things go wrong you have some back-up or support from your dealer.

The chain store vs the specialist computer supplier

Simply put, the specialist shop will usually give you better after-sales service, which is very valuable indeed. If your budget will stretch to their prices, then this is usually the best way to go. If, however, you are on a tight budget, you may prefer to buy from a chain store and then find yourself a good technical person to help you when you need it.

A useful thing to know is that lesser-known PC brand names are not necessarily inferior to the well-known ones. Most of the components are mass-manufactured in the same factories, so the PC with a brand name and the PC without a well-known name may well have exactly the same components inside. For example, a Pentium processor is a Pentium processor, no matter what brand name is on the PC tower. So ask a few questions and you'll find it's not such a difficult decision to make.

What do you need?

As a rule of thumb, always choose the fastest and 'biggest' computer you can afford. The reason is that programs are constantly being upgraded and becoming more sophisticated, and you need a PC that will be able to handle fancier software over time.

So don't buy 'small' because you think that's all you need. Buy for the future, because in the computer world the future comes surprisingly quickly.

THE VARIOUS COMPONENTS

Let's briefly look at each component so that when the people at the computer store throw all their PC jargon at you, you'll at least have an idea of what they're talking about.

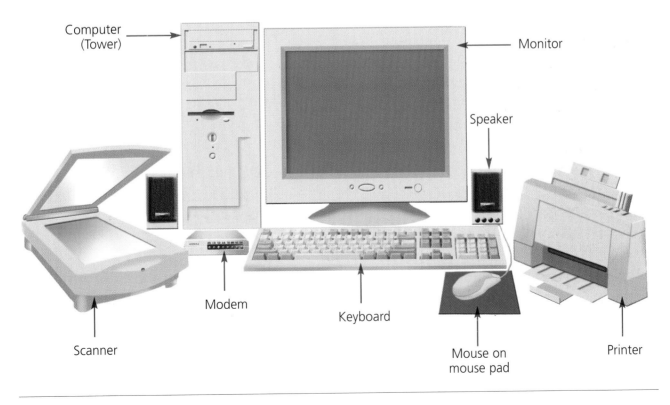

Computer (Tower)   Monitor   Speaker   Modem   Keyboard   Scanner   Mouse on mouse pad   Printer

THE COMPUTER ITSELF

Central Processing Unit (CPU)

This is the brain of the computer. The power of the CPU is measured in megahertz (MHz). This can vary from 200–750 MHz and even higher. As already mentioned, get the best you can afford. Some guidelines are included later. We recommend that you make sure it's at least a Pentium.

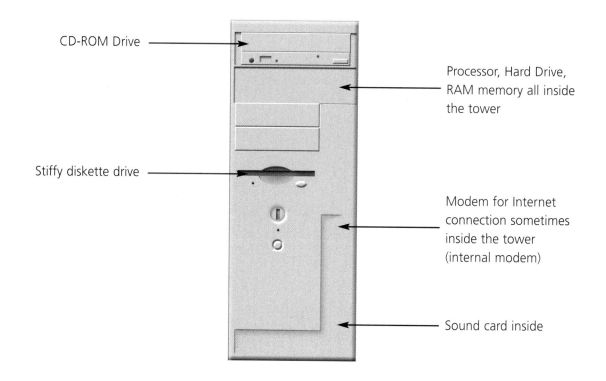

CD-ROM Drive

Processor, Hard Drive, RAM memory all inside the tower

Stiffy diskette drive

Modem for Internet connection sometimes inside the tower (internal modem)

Sound card inside

The Hard Drive

This is the amount of storage space the computer has, and it's measured in gigabytes or 'gigs'.

The hard drive must hold the **Windows** operating system, all your programs, as well as all your files, and so on. So the bigger the hard drive, the faster your system will work. Hard drives typically come in sizes ranging from three gigs (which is now considered pretty small) to over 20 gigs. Three to five gigs is quite adequate for standard use, but bigger will usually be better.

Random Access Memory (RAM)

This is the space where programs are held while you are working with them. RAM is measured in terms of megabytes or 'megs'.

The RAM needs to be big enough to be able to have several things going on at once. If you don't have enough RAM, your PC will take longer to do things, and might even malfunction. You could probably get by with 32 megs, but 64 or more is recommended.

CD-ROM Drive

You use CDs to install new programs or to listen to music through your computer's sound system. You'll definitely need a CD-ROM drive, and this is generally a standard feature these days. They vary in terms of speed, but they all do pretty much the same job.

CD Writers, special drives that are used to copy information onto a CD, are also available. But these are quite fancy and you're unlikely to need one.

Fax modem

You will definitely need a modem if you want to use e-mail or the Internet, as it connects your computer via a phone line to the Internet. It can also be used to send and receive faxes through your computer.

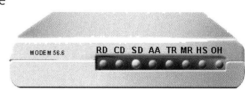

Most modern PCs already have internal modems installed, but if yours doesn't, then you can buy an external modem, which connects to your PC with a cable.

Modems vary in speed, but as the speed of transmission is finally governed by the quality of the local lines, there is a limit to how much it helps to buy a fast modem. It's like having a car that can do 200 km/h when the speed limit prevents you from going faster than 120 km/h. A 56K modem, which transmits 56 thousand bits of information per second, is recommended.

Sound cards and speakers

The sound card and speakers enable you to hear your PC's sound effects and music, and also to talk to others over the Internet, which you might want to do at a later stage. Most modern computers have speakers and sound cards installed as standard equipment.

The monitor (screen)

Monitors come in various sizes (11-inch, 13-inch, 15-inch and so on) measured diagonally across the screen. This is a personal choice – screen size determines the image quality, so ask the salesperson to show you the various options and simply choose what you can afford.

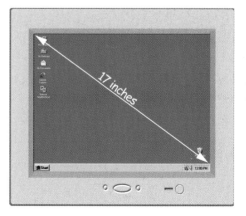

Keyboard, mouse and mouse pad

These are generally standard, although you can buy fancy versions. Usually the keyboard and mouse are part of the package. You might want to test the keyboard buttons to satisfy yourself that they have a good, solid feel to them. As far as mouse pads are concerned, the material ones are a better choice than the smoother plastic ones.

Printer

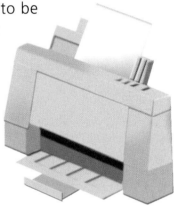

You may not need a printer at first, especially if you're going to be using your PC for e-mail. But sooner or later you will want to print things from your computer.

Colour printers are reasonably priced, and the best value for money is the ink-jet type. Laser printers are substantially more expensive, but the printing cost-per-page is less than for ink-jets. A laser printer would generally be considered unnecessary for home use.

The salesperson will advise you according to how much printing you intend to do, so be prepared for a question in this regard.

One thing to consider is that some brands, such as Hewlett Packard, have the print head mounted on the ink cartridge itself, so that every time you replace an ink cartridge you are also buying a new print head, which means good printing, but expensive ink. On other printers the print head is part of the printer itself, so the cartridges cost less. However, over time the print head gets worn and eventually needs to be replaced. This can be rather expensive on some brands. There's always a trade-off, so ask the salesperson for advice for your particular situation.

Scanner

You are unlikely to need a scanner at first. It is a photographic device that enables you to make a computer copy of documents, photos, etc. Once you've scanned something and saved it as a file, you can use it in any computer document, and can even e-mail it.

If you do want to buy a scanner, you'll probably do best to buy a 'flat-bed' model – one that has a flat surface onto which you can place your original document, much like a mini photocopier. But again, this depends on what you want to use it for.

CHECKLIST

Here's a simple checklist to help you remember the things you need to decide on when buying a computer system. You can take it with you and show the salesperson what you're looking for. The last column is for you to fill in the salesperson's suggestions.

What do I want to do on my PC?	✔
• Basic documents	
• E-mail	
• Internet	
• Accounting	
• Music CDs	
• Graphic design work	
• Creating web pages	
• Video games	
• Faxing	
My printing needs	
• Occasionally	
• Higher volume	
• Very high volume	
• Standard quality	
• Photo quality	

PC Specifications	Ballpark	Available
CPU (Pentium II, III or IV)	200 MHz upwards	
Hard Drive	5–20 GB	
RAM (memory)	64–128 K	
CD-ROM Drive	24–56 x	
Sound card	16 Bit	
Speakers		
Mouse		
Keyboard		
Modem	56K	
Operating system	Windows 2000 or later	
Wordprocessor, etc.	Office 2000 or later	
Warranty	2–3 years	
At-home service	1 year on-site	
Free phone support	Local call	
Monitor (screen)		
Colour	Super VGA	
Size (diagonally)	15–20 inch	
Printer		
Colour ink-jet or laser		
Print quality (dots per inch – 'DPI')	300–1200 DPI	
Scanner		
Size	Up to A4	
Type	Flat-bed or hand-held	

Useful info

MY FAVOURITE SHORT-CUT KEYS (Add in more as you learn them)

Documents and files

Go to a specific page	`Ctrl` + `G`	Print	`Ctrl` + `P`
Open a document	`Ctrl` + `O`	New document	`Ctrl` + `N`
Insert date	`Shift ⇧` + `Alt` + `D`	Save	`Ctrl` + `S`

Help

Help	`F1`	Spellcheck	`F7`
Find	`Ctrl` + `F`		

Cursor position

End of line	`End`	End of document	`Ctrl` + `End`
Beginning of line	`Hom`	Beginning of document	`Ctrl` + `Hom`

Alignment

Left	`Ctrl` + `L`	Centred	`Ctrl` + `E`
Right	`Ctrl` + `R`	Fill (L and R justified)	`Ctrl` + `J`

Font formats

Bold	`Ctrl` + `B`	Italics	`Ctrl` + `I`
Underline	`Ctrl` + `U`		

Copy and paste

Copy to memory	`Ctrl` + `C`	Paste here	`Ctrl` + `V`

Cut and paste

Cut text	`Ctrl` + `X`	Paste here	`Ctrl` + `V`

E-MAIL ADDRESSES I USE

Name   E-mail address

....

....

....

....

....

....

....

....

....

MY FAVOURITE INTERNET SITES

Name   Website address http://www.

....

....

....

....

....

....

....

....

....

MY LOG-ON DETAILS

For   User name   Password

....

....

....

....

....

Index